MEN-AT-ARMS SERIES

EDITOR: MARTIN WINDROW

U. S. Infantry Equipments 1775-1910

Text by PHILIP KATCHER

Colour plates by BRYAN FOSTEN

OSPREY PUBLISHING LONDON

Published in 1989 by
Osprey Publishing Ltd
59 Grosvenor Street, London W1X 9DA
© Copyright 1989 Osprey Publishing Ltd

British Library Cataloguing in Publication Data
Katcher, Philip, *1941–*
    U.S. Infantry equipments 1775–1910.—(Men-at-
    arms)
    1. United States. Army. Infantry History
    I. Title   II. Fosten, Bryan   III. Series
    356'.11'0973

ISBN 0-85045-936-2

Filmset in Great Britain
Printed through Bookbuilders Ltd, Hong Kong

Artist's Note

Readers may care to note that the original paintings
from which the colour plates in this book were
prepared are available for private sale. All
reproduction copyright whatsoever is retained by the
publisher. All enquiries should be addressed to:

Bryan Fosten
5 Ross Close,
Nyetimber,
Bognor Regis,
E. Sussex, PO21 3JW

The publishers regret that they can enter into no
correspondence upon this matter.

Introduction

The development of US Army infantry equipment has been a story of trial and error, of adopting new designs to meet new problems. It was not until 1910 that a whole system of equipment, including everything from the waist belts to the canteens to the cartridge-carriers to the haversack, was officially adopted. Prior to that, each piece of equipment was designed to meet a specific need, without any consideration of anything else the soldier had to carry. This is true even of so-called 'systems' that were developed and tested—but not adopted—by the Army from time to time during and after the Civil War.

The best example of this tendency developed during the period covered by this book is the 'system' developed by Col. William D. Mann, 7th Michigan Cavalry. In 1863 he patented a very modern-looking assembly of cartridge boxes and belts, with variations for infantry and cavalry which he attempted to sell to the Army. As it turned out, results from field tests were mixed and the system was not adopted. The point, however, is that the Mann 'system' was nothing more than a collection of cartridge boxes and belts, with no provision made for haversacks, canteens, or knapsacks. It was not a whole integrated system; the Army tried several more integrated systems in the years that followed but did not adopt one of them. The appearance of a true system had to wait until the early 20th century.

With the introduction of integrated systems in this century, model designations also came into use. These designations have, after the fact, been applied to earlier issued equipment—e.g., the 'M1858 canteen'. In the 1860s the Army did not refer to this canteen as the M1858; this is a modern affectation for ease of description. Such modern designations are used in this book, but sparingly, and only where the object has been given such a designation over such a period of time and by so

An American Soldier.

This American soldier was drawn by an eyewitness in northern New York in 1778. With his grey coat with yellow cuffs and lapels, he may represent the 7th or 12th Massachusetts Regiments. His bayonet belt and scabbard are all-black and hang from his right shoulder to his left side, while his all-black cartridge box and belt cross the other way. (New York Public Library)

British spy Charles Hamilton Smith drew these US infantrymen in New York in 1816 wearing the uniform adopted in 1813. Their belts are white, and there appears to be an oval design on the M1808 cartridge box flap. Although the ensign (second left) wears the correct shoulder belt for his sword, the other officer wears a waist belt with a plain white metal belt plate over his sash—rare at this time. (Houghton Library, Harvard University)

This 1841 print by Philadelphia publishers Huddy and Duval shows an infantry captain in full dress with a silver sword and belt plate. Note his plumed Shako with the American eagle shako plate. (Author's collection)

Company H, 44th Indiana Infantry Regiment, c.1863—a study of typical field infantry of the Civil War. The officer, second from left, wears a shoulder sling as part of his sword belt. The first sergeant, next to him, wears a common private's belt and kit, as do the other men in the company. (National Archives)

many people that it has become a *de facto* general designation.

There have been times when American soldiers have been ragged and hungry, but they have rarely lacked basic infantry equipment. Indeed, a Connecticut sergeant, Joseph Plumb Martin, recalled that when his regiment mustered at a particularly low time for American arms in 1777: 'Here we drew our arms and equipments. Uncle Sam was always careful to supply us with these articles, even if he could not give us anything to eat, drink, or wear.'

The issued equipment, however, did not meet with universal approval. A Massachusetts volunteer of 1861, Warren Lee Gross, described his feelings when marching off to war:

'Our dress consisted of a belt about the body, which held a cartridge box and bayonet, a cross belt, also a haversack and tin drinking-cup, a canteen, and, last but not least, the knapsack strapped to the back. The straps ran over, around,

and about one, in confusion most perplexing to our unsophisticated shoulders, the knapsack constantly giving the wearer the feeling that he was being pulled over backward. My canteen banged against my bayonet, both tin cup and bayonet badly interfered with the butt of my musket, while my cartridge box and haversack were constantly flopping up and down—the whole jangling like loose harness and chains on a runaway horse.'

Gradually, soldiers in each of America's wars would learn to modify the issue equipment for maximum comfort and efficiency.

Blankets, Ponchos, Shelter Halves

Blankets issued during the War of American Independence varied in colour and design. In 1776 the Army advertised for 'Blankets, striped, white, brown or mixed.'

A white blanket carried by Pte. Henry Marble during the War of Independence is in the collection of the Museum of the Fur Trade, Chadron, Nebraska. It measures 53 in. by 72 in. with a $2\frac{3}{4}$ in.

indigo blue stripe on each end, and 'points'. Points, in this case three, are narrow lines several inches long running parallel to one edge, which indicated the value of the blanket.

A list of Army supplies purchased between 1 May 1812 and 20 October 1812 included 22,276 'Rose blankets' and 17,980 'Point blankets.' Rose blankets were defined by Purveyor of Public Supplies Tench Cox in 1807 as being 'white, excepted for two roses in the smaller and four roses in the larger, wrought in with red, green and yellow yarn.' He further indicated that most point blankets were '$2\frac{1}{2}$ points'.

In 1821 Commissary General of Purchases Callender Irvine suggested, to avoid the problem of soldiers selling their blankets, 'having all Army blankets marked in the center thereof with the letters 'U.S.' with indelible liquid.' This suggestion does not appear to have been carried out until some years later.

On 12 December 1836 Irvine wrote to a supplier that 'the blankets required for the Soldiers are to be 6 feet 6 inches long and five wide to be twilled, to be made of good wool, to have the nap well raised upon them on one side, and a little raised on the other, and each blanket is to weigh 4 pounds—also to have a blue stripe on each end, of indigo, about three inches wide—otherwise the blankets are to be white & perfectly clear of all foreign matter.'

Paintings by eyewitness James Walker of the US Army in Mexico in 1847–48 show most to have carried grey blankets, some shown with what appears to be a wide blue or brown stripe on one edge. Many blankets also appear to be sky blue, with a few scarlet blankets, usually worn horseshoe-roll style by officers.

The Army's 1851 Regulations called for a grey wool blanket 'with the letters "U.S." in black, four inches long, in the centre; to be seven feet long, and five and a half feet wide, and to weigh five pounds.' An example of the type of blanket described in 1851 can be found in the Tøjhusmuseet, Copenhagen, Denmark; this was sent as part of a military equipment exchange. It was apparently from a lot bought under contract in 1857. The colour is a greyish-brown, with a black stripe $3\frac{1}{2}$ in. wide and $3\frac{3}{4}$ in. from one edge.

Blanket specifications issued in January 1885 called for a blanket of the same size but to be 'blue

This Spanish–American War period private wears a full field kit, the poncho worn as a horseshoe roll being thinner than it would be in the field when filled with tent poles, extra clothing, and a blanket. The tin cup buckled to the bottom of the haversack was issue and bore the letters 'U.S.' stamped on the handle. The weapon is the M1898 Krag rifle. (Author's collection)

7

The black letters 'US' in the centre of the M1851 blanket were chain-stitched in three parallel rows, as shown by this example. The blanket was a brownish grey. (Author's collection)

and white mixed . . . with a dark-blue stripe two and one-half to three inches wide across each end to about six inches from edge. . . . The blue color in both warp and filling to be of *pure indigo dye* of best quality of indigo. . . .

'Each blanket to have the letters "U.S." four inches long in the center, placed lengthwise with the blanket. The letters to be of pure indigo dye, and to conform in color to the stripe, and may be either woven into the fabric or stamped on the blanket.'

The blanket was often worn from the left shoulder to the right hip, rolled up in horseshoe form; the first examples of this practice seem to be among officers of the Mexican–American War. After 1861 the blanket was rolled with a rubber poncho and, shortly thereafter, half a tent.

On 1 November 1861 the Secretary of War called for 'waterproof blankets' to be issued to all soldiers. These were either painted with a black, tar-like mixture, or had a rubberised surface. The latter type, although more expensive, was more common. Veteran John Billings described this poncho as being 'vulcanized India-rubber, sixty inches wide and seventy-one inches long, having an opening in the centre lengthwise of the poncho, through which the head passes, with a lap three inches wide and sixteen inches long.' Quartermaster Department specifications for the rubber blanket dated January 1889 stated that should be 45 in. by 72 in. with 18 brass grommets evenly placed around the edges, four on each end, six on one side and eight on the other. It was to weigh $2\frac{1}{2}$ pounds.

A final component of the horseshoe roll, issued at

Two shelter halves assembled into a tent, as shown in the Quartermaster's 1889 book of specifications. Each man carried one tent pole, three pegs, and half the tent. (Author's collection)

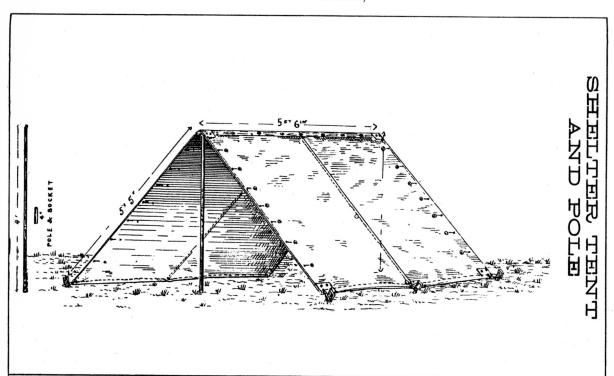

SHELTER TENT AND POLE

the same time as the poncho, was half a shelter tent. Billings said this was made of 'cotton drilling' and was 5ft 2 in. long by 4ft 8 in. wide; in 1864 a new version 5ft 6 in. by 5ft 5 in. appeared. They came with nine zinc or tin buttons on the top edge and seven on the end. There were 23 buttonholes on the upper edge and side; three loops were attached to each end. A six-thread Manila line 6ft 10 in. long came with each shelter half. Two men together could make one small tent for field use. The 1889 shelter half was to be made of cotton duck 66 in. long and 65 in. wide. Originally the men had to find their own poles or use muskets stuck in the ground by their bayonets. However, in March 1879 each man received two wooden poles, 3ft 10 in. long which were joined by a tin socket 4 in. long.

The American Army used tin canteens like this, copied from late 18th century British Army examples, as late as 1814, even though they had been dubbed obsolete by the 1790s. (Author's collection)

Canteens and Water Bottles

At the outbreak of the War of American Independence the British Army, the American model for their own army, used tin canteens. These were made like a flask, kidney-shaped or oval in cross section, and were carried over the soldier's haversack, hanging from his right shoulder to his left side. British regimental orders indicate that they were often painted with the individual soldier's rank and weapon number.

Because of material and skilled labour shortages, however, relatively few tin canteens were made for American forces. Maryland did make some, and Pennsylvania found a source of them to issue its men, but most issue canteens were made of a much more common material—wood. Those which were made, however, were in stores, listed as *old* canteens as late as 1793.

The so-called 'cheese-box' canteen used during the War of 1812 was made of wood and painted black with red letters on one side. Three leather loops are nailed to the sides; a carrying sling passed through them. (Smithsonian Institution)

Wooden canteens were made by coopers and looked like small kegs, some 6 to 9 in. in diameter. Two wooden interlocked hoops or bands, generally made of hickory or willow, held the sides together; the sides were made of staves some 3 to $4\frac{1}{2}$ in. wide. Leather, or sometimes metal loops were nailed to the sides and bottom to allow a leather or cloth shoulder sling to pass around the canteen. The canteen would carry about a quart of water.

Towards the end of the War a slightly different style of wooden canteen was developed. This replaced the staves and loops on the sides with a single piece of wood which passed all around the canteen and was then fastened together, usually with wooden pegs. It is generally known today as the 'cheesebox' canteen, after the wooden boxes in which cheese was traditionally kept.

This style became the standard by the War of 1812, when US Army issue canteens were made this way. They were painted blue-black with the red Roman letters 'U.S.' on one side. A representative sample of these canteens is $8\frac{1}{4}$ in. in diameter and $2\frac{5}{8}$ in. thick. It has three leather loops nailed on the sides for a leather or cloth sling. There is no large mouthpiece; the wood stopper is simply stuck into a hole bored into the top of the side board.

Some militia units, who had to acquire their own equipment, made copies of these canteens from tinned iron during the War of 1812.

The years after the War of 1812 were years of experiments with different types of canteens. Wooden ones were not terribly successful: they rotted out if constantly filled with water, and if left unfilled they tended to dry out so that they leaked very badly when finally refilled.

Nevertheless, most soldiers received wooden canteens. After the War of 1812, however, makers returned to something like the first keg style, but using iron bands instead of the wooden bands around the sides; these iron bands held in three iron loops for the carrying slings. A low spout was also added. These canteens were generally painted a dark blue-grey, often with white Roman letter unit designations or 'U.S.' painted on one side.

The Army also experimented with indiarubber canteens; the shape resembled a modern hot water bottle, with two indiarubber carrying loops on the upper shoulders of the canteen. The mouth was brass, as was the top of the cork. The drawback to the indiarubber canteen was the terrible taste that it gave to water carried in it.

Finally, the Army tested tin canteens made like those that had been carried by some militia units since the War of 1812; these, however, were stamped on the sides with large Roman letters 'US'. Their drawback was the fact that the water in them tended, when exposed to the sun for any time, to get unpleasantly hot.

The Army fought the Mexican–American War with all three types of wood, rubber, and tin canteens in use, the wooden one being the most common.

The M1858 canteen

In 1858 the Army adopted its first official model of canteen. This was an oblate spheroid, looking, as one soldier put it, something like a 'squashed cannonball'. It was $7\frac{3}{4}$ in. in diameter and $2\frac{3}{4}$ in. thick. Made of two tin dish-like sides soldered together, it had three tin loops, one on each upper side and one on the bottom, through which a cotton carrying sling passed. The capacity was three quarts. The spout was pewter and the cork was retained by means of an iron rod ending with an eye which passed through the cork and had a chain hooked to it from one sling loop. Many of these canteens made during the American Civil War used cotton strings, for economy's sake, to replace the chain. The Army solved the overheating problems by having the M1858 canteen covered with blanket wool. The Army's first order, some 20,000, came covered with sky blue wool; later lots were covered in dark blue, tan, or grey wool.

These canteens were well thought of and useful—in more than one respect. Many Civil War soldiers put such a canteen in a fire to melt its soldered seams away, thus making two improvised frying pans. Many Confederate soldiers tried to lay hands on the US issue canteen, to replace the motley collection of tin drum and wooden keg styles issued by their army. The M1858 did have a problem, however, in that the sides were easily bent if accidentally sat on or otherwise crushed. In 1862 the Army improved the design by having a series of concentric circles stamped into the sides, to make the body more rigid. It did have that effect, but an unintended result was that the seams split much more easily than before. By 1865, therefore, this 'bullseye' version of the M1858 canteen had been abandoned.

The M1858 was the standard issue canteen until a variation was adopted in 1879. The M1879 was essentially the same as the M1858 save that the three loops were replaced by two triangular iron sling hook fittings on the upper shoulders of the canteen, to engage with a brass hook at each end of

(Right) one type of wooden canteen, painted a bluish grey, used during the Mexican War and until replaced by (left) the M1858 tin canteen. This M1858 is covered with sky blue wool and has an inspector's mark on the white cotton sling. (Author's collection)

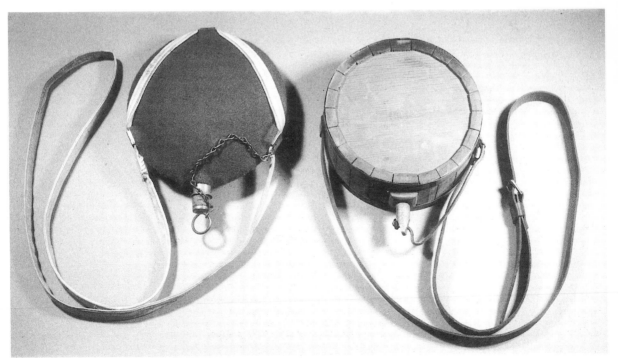

Many M1858 canteens were converted to the M1872 type, as shown here, by replacement of the sling loops and recovering. The covering here is khaki canvas cotton with black stamped letters. The adjustable sling is brown leather. (Author's collection)

a brown leather sling. The wool covering was now replaced by tan or, slightly later, khaki cotton drill. The black Roman letters 'U.S.' were printed on one side of this covering. Finally, the chain used to retain the cork was replaced by a more elaborate copper type. This was the canteen that saw use through the later Indian Wars and the Spanish–American War, finally being replaced in 1910.

Cartridge Boxes

In 1775 paper musket cartridges came as one piece, powder and ball wrapped together. These were most easily kept from weather, and the dangers of banging together and tearing open, in leather pouches with some kind of internal container, usually a piece of wood with a hole bored for each cartridge.

A Congressional Resolution passed on 19 March 1778 described the regulation cartridge box: 'The cartridge boxes to be made to hold at least 29 rounds of cartridges when made with ounce balls, and the cover of good substantial leather with a small cover or flap under it that the ammunition may be most effectually guarded against the rain. That in case any State they have quantities of tin, instead of the cartouch boxes, an equal number of tin cartridge cannisters be furnished agreeably to a pattern or description to be sent to the Board of War.'

The box described was little more than a leather bag holding a wooden block bored with 29 holes, which was carried on a white linen or white or brown leather sling from the soldier's right shoulder to his left hip. At times even the sling could be abandoned. The Army's Inspector-General Timothy Pickering recommended an expedient of providing 'cartridge boxes made of close wood (as maple or beech) with no other covering than a good leather flap nailed to it at the back near the upper edge, and of sufficient breadth to cover the top and whole front of the box; they are fixed to the body by a waist belt, which passes through two loops that are nailed to the front of the box.'

Indeed, many officers complained about the quality of the issue boxes. One described receiving an issue of cartridge boxes, many of which were 'without straps, others without flaps, and scarce any of them would preserve the cartridges in a moderate shower of Rain—what straps there are to the boxes are of linen.'

In desperation, some states adopted Congress's suggestion of providing tin canisters to hold cartridges. The Army's new Inspector-General von Steuben reported on 27 February 1778 that 'The pouches are quite as bad as the arms. A great many men have tin boxes instead of pouches.' Congress sent a circular to state quartermasters in late 1777 describing these cannisters:

'They are to be six inches and a half deep, or long; three inches and three quarters of an inch broad (this breadth receiving the cartridges lengthways, as they lie in a horizontal position) and two inches and seven eighths of an inch thick; (this thickness admitting four cartridges, to lay side by side) a box of these, in the clear, will well contain thirty six cartridges with ounce balls. A wire is to be fixed in all the edges at the top and then each side turned down (outwards) a full half inch and soldered. The cover is to be a full half inch deep, so that when fixed on the cannister the edges shall come close down to the edge formed by the inclosed wire. This cover at one end turns on a hinge being an inch and a quarter long, the wire (fixed as above mentioned) being laid naked, that space, for the purpose; and a piece of tin is run underneath the wire, doubled together, and soldered on the inside of one end of the cover. The soldier carries a cannister by a shoulder belt, as he does a cartridge box; and for this reason the cannister has fixed to it three loops of tin, each half an inch wide, with the edges turned back, to be smooth and strong; one of them is placed underneath the middle of the bottom, and one on each of the narrowest sides, the latter at four inches distant from the bottom to their lower edges. The loops are to be sent down at each end and very well soldered, leaving a space to admit a leathern belt one inch and a half wide, and nearly an eighth of an inch thick. The covers opens against one part of the belt, which causes it to fall down, after a cartridge is taken out, by which means the rest are secured from accidental fire. If possible, the cannisters should be japanned, or painted, to preserve them from rust; and all fixed to belts.'

A surviving original example in the West Point Museum had been painted black, and differs from this description only in that the top is made to open to the back, against the body, instead of to the side.

According to Army orders of 16 August 1778: 'The Tin Cannisters are to be put into the hands of those men who are in the light Infantry.' The light infantry formed the élite of American infantry at the time.

Wartime experience led to the adoption of a cartridge box described by Inspector Col. John Whiting in 1809: 'The best model of a Cartridge Box is that established by long use in the revolution, and will contain 29 rounds in the wood, 11 in the tin at the bottom, which also has a compartment

The typical cartridge box of 1775–1783 was nothing more than a leather bag containing a wooden block, bored to hold a varying number of cartridges; the block was nailed into the pouch. (George Neumann Collection, Valley Forge National Military Park)

for spare flints—on the outside a receptacle for oilcloth, worms, & screwdriver—a large flap which secures the whole from rain & supported by a Shoulder Belt.'

The box in use immediately after the Revolution, however, used a narrow belt that passed around the soldier's neck, and slipped on to a waist belt, rather than being worn on a shoulder belt. This issue box was described in November 1798 by Army Inspector Maj. Thomas Cushing: 'The Cartridge Box is made of common Harness, or Saddlers leather, and in a manner which neither secures ammunition against the weather, or gives a military appearance to the soldier. It is suspended by a black leather strap, from the soldier's neck to the waistband in front, and there is confined by another Strap round the waist. The wood part is calculated for [left blank] cartridges, & covered with a leather flap, which not being jack'd or

It was cheap and easy to provide cartridge 'boxes' that, like this example, were nothing more than a block of wood bored to hold cartridges with two loops for a waist belt nailed to the front, and a leather flap to provide at least minimal protection in foul weather. (Author's collection)

otherwise prepared, so as to turn water, yields little or no security against Rain; and it is believed that as much ammunition would be wasted in one year of active service, with these defective Boxes, would purchase new ones every way suitable to the service.'

The 1808 box

In 1808 there appeared a cartridge box with a wooden block on top, bored to hold some 26 cartridges, and a separate tin underneath to hold an additional 12 in two separate compartments of six each, along with a third, middle compartment for flints and oil rags. The box was made with a small leather flap covering an opening in the front of the box so that the soldier could reach into the tin under the block without removing the block.

The box was suspended from a belt some $2\frac{1}{2}$ in. wide, from the soldier's left shoulder to his right hip. The first belts appear to have been black, but by 1810 they were made of white buff leather. A plain oval brass plate was worn on the centre of the shoulder belt until 1819, when a brass plate with

the letters 'U.S.' cast on its face appeared. This was in turn replaced by a stamped brass circular plate bearing the design of the national eagle in 1828. Due to shortages, many of these belts were made from dyed black leather rather than of buff during the American War of 1812. These belts remained in service at least into 1817.

The box itself was some $5\frac{1}{4}$ in. tall, $8\frac{1}{2}$ in. wide, and $2\frac{1}{2}$ in. deep. The flap was some $9\frac{1}{2}$ in. wide; a single row of stitches was used to attach the leather closure tab. It had a single strap with two loops on the back through which the shoulder strap passed, and two iron buckles on the bottom to which the shoulder strap was attached.

In the 1820s the Army began adding a semi-circular piece of leather to each flap side, to add protection against driving rain coming in from the sides. This addition was retained for all future model cartridge boxes. A varnished linen cover was added between the wooden block and outer cover for additional weather protection in 1828. This was changed to a thin leather flap in 1839.

In 1832 the capacity of the lower tin in the box was enlarged to 24 cartridges, something made possible through improved gunpowder which resulted in smaller cartridges.

At that time, too, the plain flap of the box was altered, pressed into a mould so that the edges were finished with a floral border, and an oval in the centre of the flap surrounded an eagle and the Roman letters 'US'. A ribband over the oval bore the motto E PLURIBUS UNUM ('from many, one'). The design was slightly changed in 1834, with the letters 'US' being dropped from the oval. However, varnish tended to hide this elaborate design, and by 1836 cartridge boxes were again being made with plain flaps. In 1839, due to the weight of a loaded box, the lower tin capacity was reduced to 16 rounds, giving a total of 42 rounds in a fully loaded box. The desire to mark the flap in some way persisted, however; and the 1841 *Ordnance Manual* called for a 'plate, brass, oval $3\frac{1}{2}$ in. by $2\frac{1}{5}$ in. lettered 'U.S.' for the box flap.

With the adoption of a percussion-cap rifle in 1842, a new cartridge box was issued. This was the first issued box to eliminate the wooden block, having instead two internal tin containers arranged side by side. Each container held ten rounds vertically on top, and a paper-wrapped package of

The M1808 cartridge box was marked by a small flap inside that opened to allow entry to the tin under the wooden block above. The finial was a leather tab, rather than being made of metal. (Author's collection)

another ten cartridges below. The top section was divided, holding five rounds in each section, so that the remaining rounds would not fall over after several had been removed. The box also came with a small pouch on the inside front, under the outer flap, in which the soldier could carry rifle tools, patches for cleaning, and an oil rag.

In 1850 another box for percussion-cap rifles was adopted; very similar in exterior appearance to the M1842 box, it differed in several important aspects. The internal tin was made as a single piece, with one large tray on the bottom and five sections on the top. Moreover, on the external back surface, where in previous boxes a single horizontal strip of leather had formed two loops for a shoulder belt, the M1850 box had two vertical straps forming loops for use on the waist belt; the M1850 box could not be carried on a shoulder belt. The implement pouch on the inside box front was eliminated from this model.

The M1855 box

A new box incorporating the best of the M1842 and M1850 models was introduced with the adoption of the M1855 rifled musket. This box returned to

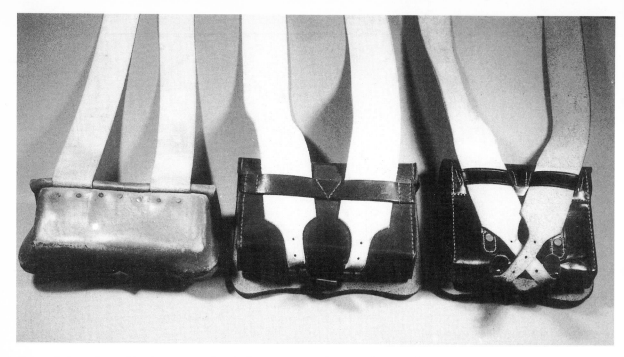

The evolution of cartridge box suspension: (left) a War of Independence model with linen straps nailed into the box itself; the M1808 model (centre) was designed to be carried on a shoulder strap that could be buckled and unbuckled for height adjustment or removal; the M1855 box (right) had loops for both shoulder and waist belts. (Author's collection)

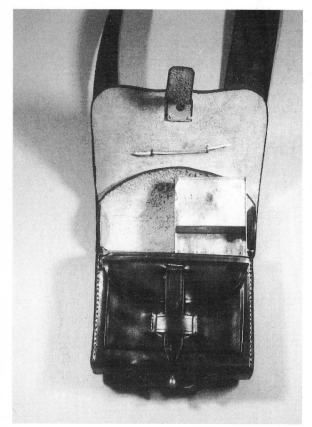

The M1855 cartridge box opened with one tin pulled up. The strip of rawhide lace at top secures the brass cartridge box plate. The pouch on the inside of the box held patches, rags, and musket tools. (Author's collection)

the two tin containers holding 40 rounds, 20 rounds vertically at the top and 20 underneath in packets, and the implement pouch on the inside front. Moreover, it had both horizontal loops for use on a shoulder belt and vertical loops for a waist belt. In Civil War practice, many Zouave regiments carried their M1855 boxes on their waist belts, but most other commands required the box to be carried on the black shoulder belt with its circular brass plate.

The adoption of the brass fixed cartridge in 1866 for the regulation Infantry shoulder arm rendered obsolete the hundreds of thousands of M1855 boxes the Army had acquired during the Civil War. Brass cartridges tended to bang around too much in the tins. Rather than simply scrap all these boxes, the Army retained and converted them, for the new cartridges. This was done in several ways. In the first, the tin liners were removed and replaced with sheepskin. Two cartons of cartridges, each holding 20 rounds, could be fitted into this box. The Army also returned to the wooden block system, issuing wooden blocks with holes for 20 cartridges to replace the pair of tins. These came in both long versions that filled the entire box, and short versions that fitted on top of each other in the M1855 box. The problem, however, was that concentrating all the ammunition's weight—some 5lb—was very uncomfortable for the soldier.

Field experience underlined the fact that soldiers preferred a cartridge belt to a box once brass fixed ammunition became standard. However, the Army hierarchy preferred the traditional cartridge box. First Lieutenant Samuel McKeever, 2nd Infantry Regiment, patented a box that held 40 rounds of the new type of ammunition on 10 January 1873. With some changes, mostly to make it smaller, it was adopted as the standard the following year.

The M1874 box was made of black leather with two sides, connected at the bottom with a brass rod. Loops on either side held ten cartridges, for a total of 20 cartridges in a box. A brass finial on one side was hooked into a leather tab on the other side to keep the box closed when not in action. The box was 6½ in. long, by 3¼ in. deep, by 1½ in. wide. Two boxes, one on either side of the waist belt plate, were to be worn at the same time; for dress, one would be worn in the centre of the back.

A new pattern appeared in 1885 which eliminated the brass escutcheon that had surrounded the slit in the flap, and the brass clips from the ends. Duck replaced the russet leather on to which the loops were initially sewn. With the introduction of 0.30 calibre ammunition an M1903 McKeever box appeared, this one 5½ in. long.

The Army may have liked the McKeever box; its soldiers did not. Capt. F. Heath, commanding the Cheyenne Depot, wrote on 22 August 1882 that: 'The cartridge belt is, of course, invariably used in the field and garrison for all practical purposes,

The McKeever box opened to reveal web cartridge loops; the brass finial was worn at the top. (Author's collection)

such as while on guard duty, drills, target practice, etc.; the leather belt and box being used only on occasion of ceremony. At many posts the belt and box are worn on guard mounting, immediately after the ceremony the cartridge belt being substituted for them.'

The cartridge box was dead as a piece of infantry field equipment in the US Army. Even so, the McKeever box in one form or another survived, and is even today in use by cadets at the US Military Academy at West Point, and by the 3rd Infantry Regiment in Washington, DC.

Percussion Cap Pouches

One stumbling block associated with the adoption of weapons that fired with percussion caps rather than traditional flintlocks was the fear that soldiers would lose the tiny copper percussion caps. The first solution to this problem, after the adoption of the M1841 percussion-action rifle was to have small slash pockets inserted just above the waistline in the soldier's jacket; the caps could be carried in these pockets. This method was used by those soldiers lucky enough to have these modern weapons in the Mexican–American War; but problems immediately became apparent. The

constant pulling on the sides tended to tear the soldier's jacket; and as there was no flap on the pocket, caps could, and did, spill out in action.

A small black leather version of the cartridge box was adopted to contain percussion caps, and was first issued in 1850. This was made with two leather loops on the back, to be carried on the waist belt on the right front hip, next to the belt plate. According to the 1861 *Ordnance Manual*, cap pouches were made of black bridle leather, 3 in. long and deep and $1\frac{1}{4}$ in. wide. There was both an outer and an inner flap, the outer flap buttoning to the bottom with a brass finial. A strip of woolly sheepskin was glued (with fish-glue) and sewed to the inside back at the mouth of the pouch to prevent cap loss. The wire rod used to clear a fouled musket's nipple was carried in a loop in the inner left hand corner of the cap pouch. Some of these pouches were made with the outer flap being cut in a shield-shape on the bottom, with a separately sewn-on narrow leather strap that buttoned to the finial; most were simply cut with the flap ending in a point that was buttoned directly to the finial.

Cap pouches were issued for as long as percussion cap weapons, starting to be phased out in 1866.

Knapsacks

In 1775 the British Army was just beginning a long, slow change from a knapsack that was worn slung diagonally on the back from the left shoulder, partly under the right arm, to one that sat square on the back. Originally it had been nothing more than another haversack, a 'snapsack' used to carry the soldier's clothing, while his food went into the haversack; indeed, the two terms 'knapsack' and 'haversack', were often used interchangeably during the War of American Independence.

The first American knapsack—indeed, one of the first pieces of unique issue American equipment of any sort—was described on a piece of paper now found in the Maryland Archives. Dated 9 February 1776, it describes a 'newly invented Napsack and haversack in one That is adopted by

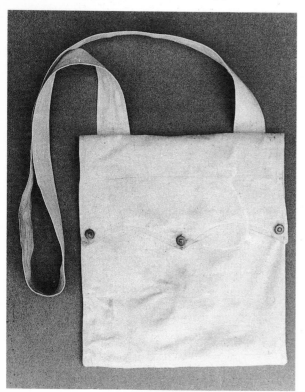

The haversack used from the beginning of the 19th century until the 1850s was made of white duck with three pewter buttons. (Author's collection)

18

the American Regulars of Pennsylvania, New Jersey & Virginia.'

An accompanying sketch shows a piece of duck 26 in. long and 21 in. wide, folded in the middle. A single leather strap, buckling in front for size adjustment, passes from one point where the duck is folded in half to the other. Three small leather straps placed evenly along one edge engage with three small buckles on the other. The outside was said to have been painted red, with a separate piece of linen sewn all around its edges. A slot in the middle, probably tied shut with rawhide laces, enabled the soldier to store clothing in this, the knapsack section of the device. A piece of Russian linen made a bag which was open at the top on the other side for the haversack portion. The whole thing was apparently worn over the right shoulder, under the left arm, on the back.

Americans also wore knapsacks square on the back, with straps passing over both shoulders, made of duck or goatskin. This was the style—in canvas, with outer flaps painted Spanish brown or red and usually decorated with a unit designation—that remained in use after the war. The 1st US Infantry Regiment of 1790 had knapsack flaps covered with bearskin.

Maj. Thomas Cushing reported to the Army's Inspector-General in November 1798 on the issue knapsack: 'The Knapsack is made of coarse linen or Duck, with a painted cover or flap, and answers very well in dry weather; but does not defend the soldiers Clothing and necessaries against Rain. There has been a great deficiency of this article for some years, and you will seldom see a detachment on a march, in which many of the soldiers are not obliged to substitute the Blanket (as a roll) for the Knapsack.'

In March 1808 the Army ordered 4,000

Typical contents are shown with this tar-coated haversack of the Civil War period. They are, from top left, clockwise: a leather case holding two photographs, a razor, and a deck of cards printed in New York. Photographed on the white cotton food-bag which buttoned inside the haversack are a wood tompion (muzzle plug) under a piece of lye soap, a knife, fork, and spoon, a 'housewife' filled with sewing utensils, and a toothbrush. (Author's collection)

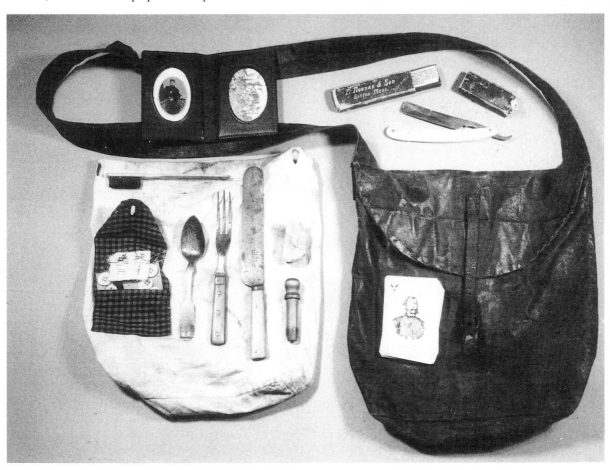

The khaki canvas haversack of the Spanish–American War period was usually marked with the owner's name. The adjustable brown leather strap was the same as that used on the canteen. (Author's collection)

M1833 knapsack; this had a cowhide flap, and a rectangular wooden internal frame some 14 by 14 in. to keep it stiff. The soldier's blanket was rolled up and worn strapped to the top with two leather straps. The back was to be marked with the Infantry horn, regimental number, and company letter in white paint.

The M1853 knapsack

This was replaced with a new model in 1853. The new knapsack was made of heavy duck, painted with a black waterproof covering—gutta percha. As with the earlier model, the blanket was to be rolled up and secured on top of the knapsack by two leather straps. However, there was no rigid frame, and the knapsack was left free to sag according to whatever it contained.

Inside, the knapsack was made as two bags. The one that was part of the outer flap had an inner flap tied shut with two pairs of rawhide laces. It was some $13\frac{1}{2}$ in. by 14 in. by 6 in. wide. The other, inner section was essentially an envelope of triangular-shaped 'ears' that buckled across each other in pairs; it was some 11 in. high by 14 in. wide. Overcoats or heavy clothing could be carried in this.

Two wide leather straps passed over the shoulder, coming together in a triangle in the rear

knapsacks, with black leather shoulder straps and Prussian blue flaps with the letters 'US' in Spanish brown. In May this latter colour was changed to vermilion, which would stand out better.

At that time, too, the Army adopted a knapsack patented by John Lherbette, a New Yorker. It was made of Russia sheeting, painted blue with red letters 'US' in a white circle on the flap. The pack was 15 in. deep, 17 in. wide, and $3\frac{1}{2}$ in. thick; it was divided in half inside, and the flap was made with a separate bag to keep wet clothing away from other clothes. A greatcoat could be strapped between the flap and the sack.

As Lherbette knapsacks wore out during the 1830s, this style, which still did not resist water as well as could be desired, was slowly replaced by an

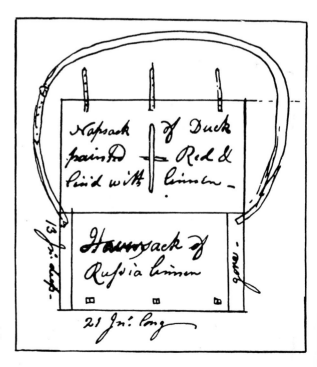

This sketch shows a type of knapsack/haversack combination apparently used by a number of Revolutionary War soldiers. (Maryland Archives)

centre of the knapsack. They were attached to narrower straps that passed under the soldier's arms and fastened to the bottom of the knapsack. Two additional narrow leather straps crossed the soldier's chest and fastened together. In 1855 the straps that passed across the chest were made with hooks that fastened into the slots in the M1855 rifleman's belt. According to regulations of 1857, infantrymen marked their outer knapsack flaps with their regimental number in white.

The M1853 knapsack served officially until 1872. In that year the Chief of Ordnance reported: 'The knapsacks on hand, left over from the war, are now worthless and unfit for issue, and will be sold as soon as they can be replaced.'

Indeed, even before 1872, whenever soldiers in the field got the chance, they stored or threw away their knapsacks and wore their spare clothing rolled up in their blanket, shelter half, or waterproof. By Chancellorsville (May 1863) some 50 per cent of the Army of the Potomac's XI and XII Corps had replaced their knapsacks with blanket rolls, as did 30 per cent of V Corps, and 25 per cent of the Army as a whole. Army of the Potomac veteran John D. Billings wrote: 'If he (the soldier) intends to take his effects in a knapsack, he will at the start have put by more to carry than if he simply takes his blankets (rubber and woollen) rolled and slung over his shoulder. Late in the war this latter was the most common plan, as the same weight could be borne with less fatigue in that manner than in a knapsack, slung on the back.'

Pte. Elisha Stockwell, Jr., 14th Wisconsin Infantry Regiment, described how these blanket rolls were made: 'We rolled our blankets up (each had a wool and oilcloth blanket), with the oilcloth on the outside, tied the two ends together, and put the roll over our heads and across the left shoulder, took our canteens and haversack, and left the camp. . .'

From 1872 until 1910 the Army experimented with a number of knapsacks, mostly as part of infantry equipment systems, but nothing more

(Above) Inside of the M1853 knapsack. An overcoat would be strapped inside the envelope on the right, while other clothing would be placed in the bag at the left. The knapsack was folded closed and buckled with the three leather straps. (Author's collection)

(Below) The black leather pouch used for carrying percussion caps came with two belt loops both sewn and riveted on for safety. A typical Ordnance Department inspector's stamping is shown on the flap of the right-hand example. (Author's collection)

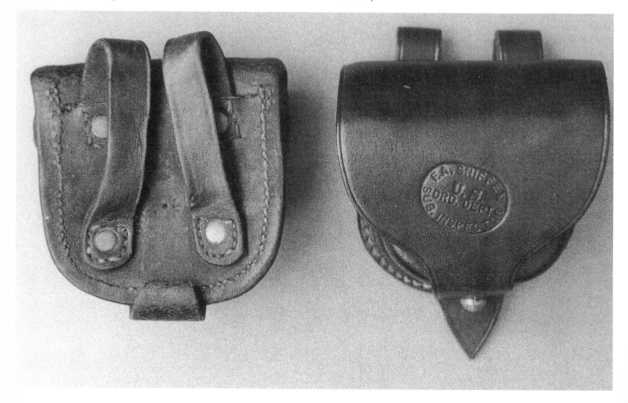

comfortable than the blanket or horseshoe roll was found. By the Spanish–American War of 1898 the Army had devised a regulation manner of rolling and wearing the horseshoe roll, as Pte. Charles Johnson Post, a New York infantryman, found:

'In the business of making a blanket roll, you lay the blanket on the ground, put into it your tent pegs and your half of the two tent poles—for each man carried but one-half the tent—and then arrange your towel, socks, shirt, and extra underwear and roll up the blanket. Then, turning your attention to your half of the tent, fold it lengthwise. This you lay on top of the blanket roll, fasten it at the ends and the middle, much as if reefing a sail, then bend it until it takes its horse-collar shape, fasten the two ends—and there you are ready to stick your head through and sling it. It is excellent. But—and this we learned on our first march to the transport—the blanket roll must be made sloppy, not neat. A hard, neat horse collar will bear into the shoulder like a steel bar, so roll it loose and floppy for the part that lies over the shoulder and with no baggage inside the center section—just at the two ends. It looks like a clumsy, amateur sausage lying out straight, but it is soft on the shoulder. In Cuba our horse collars made us look like a bunch of hobo blanket-stiffs. . .'

Waist Belts & Bayonet Scabbards

Bayonets have been carried in scabbards suspended from waist or shoulder belts since 1775. At that time the British Army carried their bayonet scabbards hooked into frogs hanging from white leather waist belts. They were, however, beginning to use these waist belts as shoulder belts, hanging from the right shoulder to the left hip. American infantry used both methods, the shoulder belt being the most popular. Both types of belts were also made with single frogs, to hold a bayonet in its scabbard; and double frogs, for a bayonet and a short sabre, or hanger, in separate scabbards. Maryland troops also received double frogs which were intended for a bayonet and a tomahawk. Since the use of hangers by soldiers below the rank of sergeant was dying out at this time, most bayonet belts came with single frogs.

As it turned out, however, the Americans were hard pressed to supply any sort of belts át all. When the Pennsylvania Division was inspected on 1 October 1779 it was found that only 1,628 men had bayonet belts, while 2,551 were lacking them. Consequently a general order appeared on 2 August 1780 stating: 'As there is a very great scarcity of Bayonet belts and scabbards, the Gen'l Directs that the Troops keep their bayonet Continualy fixed, except when Cleaning, as well as in Camp as on every kind of Duty whatsoever with arms.' When belts were supplied, they were often made of white linen, with leather frogs and attached scabbards sewn to them.

Supply problems over bayonet belts continued for years after the War of Independence. In April 1790 one infantry company was issued 90 waist belts which they were supposed to convert into shoulder belts. According to Maj. Thomas Cushing in November 1798, 'Bayonet Belts and Scabbards are not furnished' to the infantry at the time. Again, soldiers were usually ordered to keep their bayonets fixed at all times. In 1799 another order called for bayonet scabbards to be fixed to the waist belts provided with the 'belly boxes' then being issued. By the turn of the century, however, the leather bayonet belt, worn from the right shoulder to the left hip, with a plain oval pewter belt plate worn at the centre of the chest, was an item of common issue, and it remained so for the next three decades.

This is not to say that there were not shortages from time to time, especially in the early years of the century. A German visitor to America, Duke Karl Bernhard, reported seeing soldiers at New Orleans in 1826 who had 'no bayonet sheaths, nor gun straps', although they did wear 'the belt intended for the bayonet sheath over that of the cartridge box. . .'

The first belts that were issued concurrently with the M1808 cartridge boxes were made of black, rather than buff leather, $2\frac{1}{4}$ in. wide, with a $2\frac{1}{2}$ in. wide plain oval brass plate worn on the centre of the chest. The Roman letters 'U.S.' were added to the plate by 1819. The plate was used to adjust the belt for men of different heights, with a plain leather loop at the other end of the belt used to keep the two ends neatly together. Privates' belts had one frog for a bayonet scabbard; non-commissioned officers' belts had two, one for the bayonet and the other for the issue sword.

A black bayonet scabbard, with a small brass ball at the end and a brass hook at the throat, was hooked into the frog at the end of the shoulder belt. The bayonet was worn with its socket facing out until some time during the War of 1812, when the Army began issuing bayonet scabbards with the hooks made so that the bayonet sockets faced inwards.

From the beginning, white was the preferred belt colour, and Army orders as early as 1810 call for white rather than black belts. Even so, for economy reasons, black belts were used at least as often by infantry in the War of 1812; indeed, they saw use as late as 1819.

In 1828 a brass ferrule or band was added to the

Many soldiers of the War of Independence wore their bayonet scabbards on waist belts such as this one. The black scabbard has a brass hook which hooks into the white buff leather frog (which slides loose on the belt), and a brass finial at the tip. The bayonet is of British manufacture for a Brown Bess musket but bears a US surcharge over the maker's name. (Author's collection)

bayonet scabbard throat for strength. The shoulder belt, too, was changed, two frogs now being used by all grades, and a stamped brass circular belt plate with the design of an eagle replacing the oval 'U.S.' plate.

In the field, many soldiers preferred to take the weight off their shoulders and began, by the 1820s and 1830s, to attach their bayonet scabbards to a musket sling used as a waist belt. Non-commissioned officers were the first to wear waist belts by regulation. In that year they were ordered to carry the M1832 foot artillery and infantry sword—a heavy, short, straight-bladed sword similar to the contemporary French model and somewhat resembling an ancient Roman *gladius*. This sword came in a black scabbard that buttoned into a white buff-leather frog suspended from a white buff-leather waist belt. A variety of belt plates saw use with this belt. The first type used two circles which were connected by a piece of brass wire in the shape of a sideways 'S'. A national eagle motif appeared on the left circular plate, while the right one bore a stack of three muskets with fixed bayonets, with the Roman letters 'US' on either

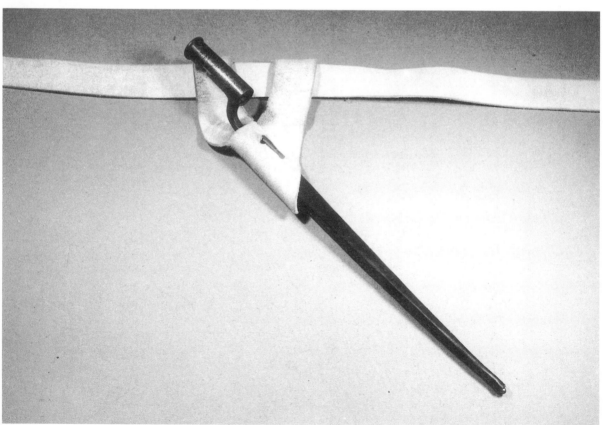

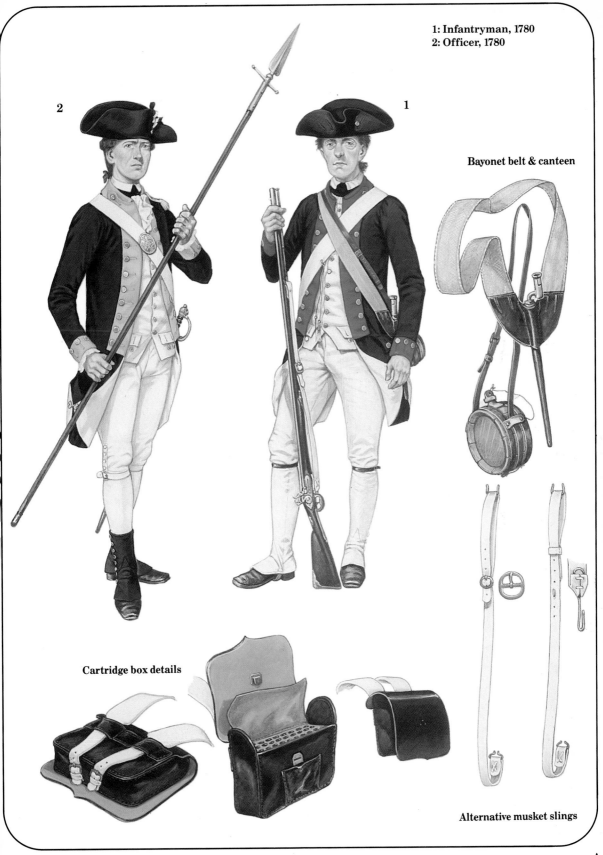

1: Infantryman, 1780
2: Officer, 1780

2

1

Bayonet belt & canteen

Cartridge box details

Alternative musket slings

A

1: Infantryman, 1813
2: Officer, 1813

Haversack & canteen

Lherbette patent knapsack, 1808

B

1: Infantryman, 1832
2: Officer, 1832

Improved 1808 cartridge
box with 1832 flap

C

1: Infantryman, 1847
2: Officer, 1847

2

1

Shoulder belt &
bayonet scabbard

M1842 cartridge box

D

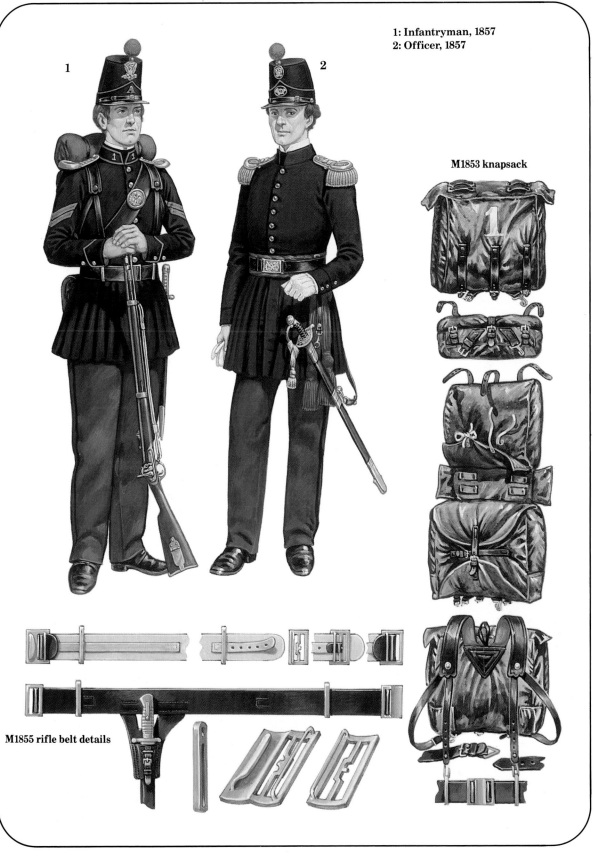

1: Infantryman, 1857
2: Officer, 1857

M1853 knapsack

M1855 rifle belt details

E

1: Infantryman, 1863
2: Officer, 1863

2

1

Haversack
& canteen

Revolver,
holster &
bayonet
scabbard

cap pouch

M1855 cartridge box

F

1: Infantryman, 1876
2: Officer, 1876

2

1

Officer's buckle
(see also Plates E, F, H)

M1860 Officer's sword

Alternative fittings

McKeever cartridge box

G

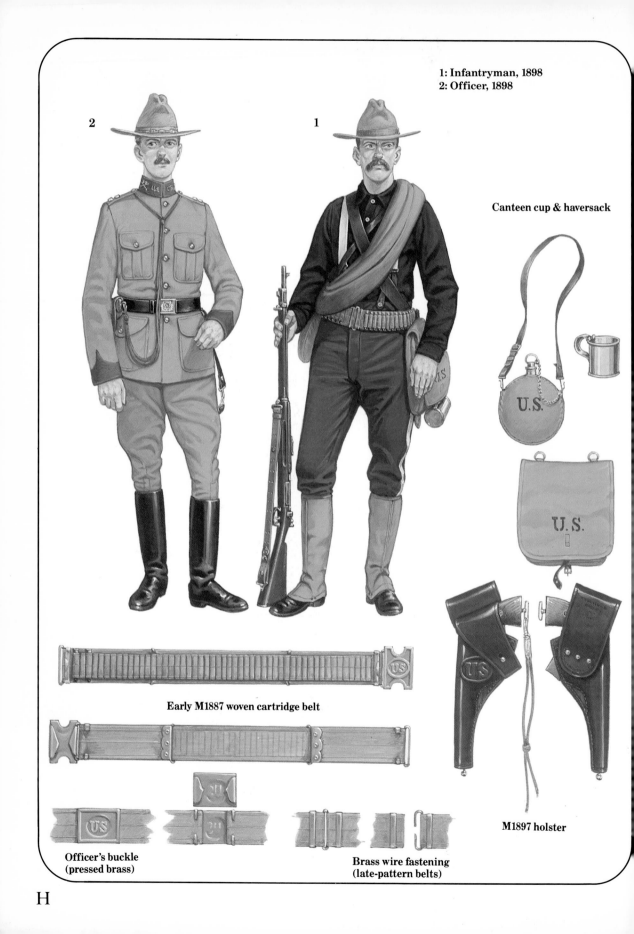

1: Infantryman, 1898
2: Officer, 1898

Canteen cup & haversack

Early M1887 woven cartridge belt

M1897 holster

Officer's buckle
(pressed brass)

Brass wire fastening
(late-pattern belts)

H

side. This lasted until 1836, when a two-piece circular belt plate, bearing the Roman letters 'US' within a circle, was first issued with this belt.

In 1840 the Army adopted a new sword for its non-commissioned officers, one with a much longer blade than the M1832. It, too, had a straight blade and came with a black leather scabbard, but it was supposed to be carried in a shoulder belt from the right shoulder to the left hip. The belt featured a circular brass plate in its centre, used for size adjustment, and two frogs, one for the sword and the other for a bayonet scabbard. M1840 non-commissioned officer sword scabbards were, in actual practice, also carried hooked into frogs worn on waist belts.

Around 1836 the practice of wearing waist belts instead of shoulder belts by all enlisted men became officially accepted in the 7th Infantry Regiment, even without War Department approval. However, the practice was so widespread and popular that the Ordnance Department began listing waist belts and waist belt plates as 'new pattern' issue items in the 1839 *Ordnance Regulations*.

The 1841 *Regulations* described these belts as being made of buff leather, $1\frac{1}{2}$ in. wide and $38\frac{1}{2}$ in. long 'with a *loop* at one end' and an oval brass plate bearing the Roman letters 'US' in the centre. This belt, too, was made of white buff leather, but in 1856 the Army had waist belts dyed black. In 1854 the loop at one end was replaced by a brass keep; this was the most common waist belt of the American Civil War. Black leather scabbards with brass tips and white buff frogs for the triangular bayonet slid onto these belts, being worn on the left hip.

In 1851, with the adoption of a rectangular belt plate bearing the design of an eagle within a silver wreath, for use by non-commissioned officers, a new black belt for this plate was also adopted. It was wider, at $1\frac{9}{10}$ in. wide, than the old infantry bayonet belt. This belt also used an adjustment system with a brass hook being placed in holes along the side, unlike previous belts which were adjusted by placing the plate hook in the appropriate hole.

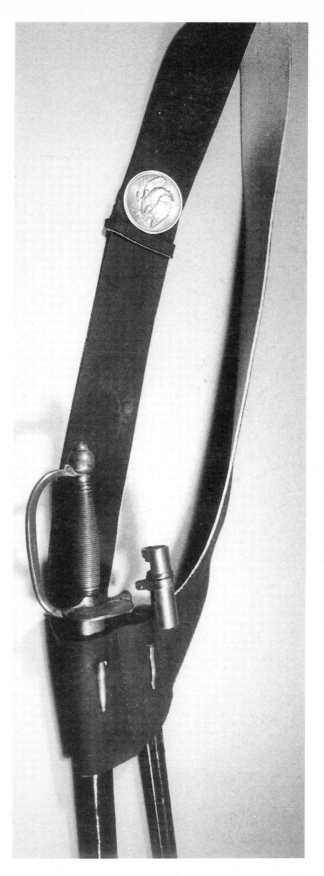

The M1840 non-commissioned officers' sword was designed to be carried in this shoulder belt, with a double frog so that the bayonet scabbard could be carried as well. The same M1828 circular plate as was worn on the cartridge box sling was worn with this belt. (Author's collection)

In 1856 all the belts and plates were made as wide as the non-commissioned officer's belt and plate. The belt loop at one end, used to keep it neat when worn, was officially replaced by a piece of sheet brass that folded around the belt at each side to secure the end. Both this type, and the older loop type, were seen during the Civil War.

At the same time the scabbard frog was changed to black leather, and given rivets for added strength. The leather scabbard itself, however, could be badly bent or broken when the bayonet was not in it. In 1862 E. J. Emerson of Trenton, New Jersey, patented a bayonet scabbard which used the same black leather, riveted frog as the M1855 scabbard, but had an all-steel sheath. The resulting scabbard was actually cheaper—by 25 cents each—and more durable than the all-leather scabbard and the Army ordered 20,000 of them in August 1862.

The basic scabbard lasted until 1870, when the Army adopted the patented Hoffman swivel. This used the same sheath and leather loop to slip around the waist belt; however, a large brass rivet, marked 'US' in its centre, held the two pieces together. The bayonet scabbard itself could be rotated around this rivet to fit the soldier more comfortably. Some 50,000 Emerson scabbards were modified to take the Hoffman swivel, and the all-steel scabbard was standard for all 45/70 bayonets.

In 1866 Capt. Anson Mills, 18th Infantry Regiment, asked the post saddler at Fort Bridger, Wyoming, to take an ordinary M1851 non-commissioned officer's leather belt and add canvas loops, each the size of one Spencer rifle metallic cartridge, around its outside. To protect each cartridge, Mills had him add a thin leather flap that covered the cartridges and was secured by small brass buttons. The flap could be lifted in sections, revealing six cartridges at a time. Mills patented this system in August 1867, and submit-

This sergeant photographed in 1861 wears his M1840 non-commissioned officers' sword on the M1851 non-commissioned officers' waist belt with a separate frog that could be slipped onto the waist belt. (Author's collection)

The evolution of the bayonet scabbard as worn on the waist belt: (left) the leather scabbard for the M1842 musket with its buff frog; (middle) the all-black scabbard for the M1855 rifled musket; (right) the steel scabbard for the .45/70 rifle with a part leather/part brass frog that hooked onto the waist belt. (Author's collection)

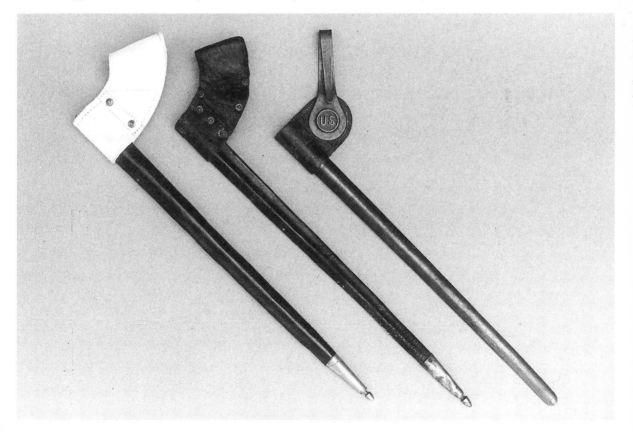

This Spanish–American War period corporal wears the M1887 cartridge belt with its 'H'-shaped buckle plate. (Author's collection)

ted it to the Army to replace the cartridge box. Leather was found to foul the cartridges, which often had to be carefully cleaned when so carried. Mills replaced the leather of his original belt with woven canvas. The men liked the new system; but the Army wanted to retain cartridge boxes.

The Army's answer to the popularity of the looped ammunition belt was to test the system designed by 1st Lt. George Palmer, 16th Infantry Regiment, which used the M1851 belt with the rectangular brass belt plate bearing the Roman letters 'US' within an oval on its face which had been adopted for the cavalry in 1872. Palmer added brass loops to the plate and belt, into which a set of leather braces attached. A McKeever cartridge box was to be worn on either side of the belt plate, the braces taking the weight off the soldier's waist. An iron bayonet scabbard with a leather frog slid on to the belt with a brass hook.

This system still used the hated cartridge box instead of the preferred cartridge belt, and hence proved unpopular. Finally, in 1876, two Ordnance inspectors reported that it was impossible to compel the soldier on the frontier to use the regulation McKeever cartridge boxes, and recommended the manufacture of a uniform belt at arsenals. The Chief of Ordnance approved, and 30,000 sewn canvas belts were made thereafter at Watervliet Arsenal.

These belts differed from previous types in that they used plain brass frame buckles. They were made of tan canvas with russet leather tongues, and came in 2 in. and $2\frac{9}{16}$ in.-wide models. Each held 54 rounds of 0.45 calibre ammunition and was $45\frac{1}{2}$ in. long, including buckle. After the first shipment they were made $2\frac{1}{2}$ in. wide, since lead bullets sticking out from the belt smudged uniforms.

As it turned out, the issue loops on the M1876 belts often stretched and became too large to hold cartridges after prolonged use. Therefore, in 1878, the Army adopted cartridge belts woven by a system Mills himself devised. The first Mills belts were not, however, issued until 1880.

In 1878 the Army also began adding rings on the belt to which to hook the bayonet scabbard.

The Army wished to use the letters 'US' on the belt plates as it had before; and in 1880 issued a web cartridge belt with a large brass buckle roughly in the form of the letter 'H' with the Roman letters

'US' within a central oval. There were some slight variations of this belt and plate thereafter. The M1880 and M1883 plates were sand-cast, but the M1885 and M1887 plates were stamped brass. These fitted belts considerably wider than the M1876 model, being 3 in. wide with $2\frac{1}{4}$ in. (average) loops for cartridges. The M1887 belts also had a brass hook for the bayonet scabbard. Starting in the 1890s these belts came with two, rather than one, rows of cartridge loops, giving them a 100-round capacity. The elaborate 'H' belt plate, was dropped during the mobilisation for the Spanish–American War in favour of a simple brass wire closure method.

In 1903 the Army adopted a new Springfield rifle which used cartridges loaded in clips of five rounds each. These obviously could not be kept in cartridge belts with loops, and a new M1903 woven infantry cartridge belt was adopted. This came with nine woven khaki pouches, each capable of holding two clips of ammunition. It used a wire hook closure method; and came with metal grommets at the bottom into which other infantry equipment—such as a bayonet, entrenching tool, and a canteen—could be hooked.

A pointed 'Spitzer' bullet was adopted in 1906, which tended to tear out the bottom of the cartridge pouches; these were made thereafter 'puckered' which solved the problem.

Rifle Equipment

Not every soldier could use prepared cartridges easily; riflemen in 1775 usually chose to carry powder horns and pouches with lead balls separately. In this way they could measure exactly how much fresh powder they needed, and cut a patch to hold the ball in the lands and grooves of the rifle.

It is no surprise to find orders such as one issued on 17 December 1778 that the 'Commissary of hides' should 'deposit all the horns of the Cattle Kill'd for the army with the Commissary of Military Stores, who is hereby Directed to have them Converted Into Powder Horns, for the use of the Troops, as fast as they are Delivered to him.'

These first pouches and horns carried by riflemen of the War of Independence were of civilian design, varying according to individual taste and means. However, William Duane's 1813 *Hand Book for Rifleman* states that a rifleman should be equipped with: 'A cartridge box of flexible leather containing two rows of tin unsoldered cases, to contain 30 or 36 rounds ball cartridge; a double pouch slung over his right shoulder and under his left arm, one partition containing 60 loose well smoothed balls, and in the other partition his turn screw, knife, scouring brush, oil rag, patches. Over his left shoulder and under his right arm hang his powder horn with the best powder.' Duane must have known whereof he spoke; he served as the lieutenant-colonel in the Regiment of Riflemen from 1808 to 1810.

This rifleman, left, wears the usual white linen rifle dress of the War of Independence. Although he wears a cartridge box, he does not carry a bayonet since they were not fitted to rifles. The infantryman he faces, apparently from the Pennsylvania Line, wears a white shoulder belt for his bayonet scabbard and another to support his cartridge box. (Anne S. K. Brown Military Collection, Brown University Library)

'Riflemen', said Duane, 'are never required to fire with cartridges but when acting in close order, which though it often happens, is not precisely their province in action. Whenever it is practicable, riflemen will load with powder measure and loose

This M1850 copper flask was designed to hook on to the outer straps of the M1841 rifle pouch and belt. It is known as the 'peace flask,' because of the clasped hands in the centre of the design. The spout is a replacement; the original had adjustments to produce different measures of powder. (Author's collection)

ball.' At the time Duane wrote, riflemen received a 3 in.-wide leather waist belt with a painted linen pouch worn in front. This was apparently used for cartridges for close formation combat. Regimental orders in the Regiment of Riflemen dated 31 October 1819 state that: 'The powder horn and pouch will be reserved for excursions or any species of actual service. . .'

The powder horn made from a cow's horn was already on the way out, however, to be replaced by a copper powder flask with an adjustable spout which poured an exact measure of powder. These came into widespread use in the 1830s, and were hung from the same strap as the pouch. The 1834 *Ordnance Regulations* called for both white buff and black belts; these were split at the ends, one $\frac{3}{4}$ in. wide strap on each end buckling on to a leather pouch and the other pair of straps on to the triangular clips of the powder flask. An oval brass plate was worn on the belt on the centre of the chest. The belt was dropped in the 1839 *Ordnance Regulations*.

The first detailed description of the issue rifle pouch appeared in the 1841 *Ordnance Regulations*, which called for a pouch that was 7 in. wide at the bottom, $6\frac{2}{3}$ in. at the top, and $5\frac{1}{2}$ in. deep. The flap was $2\frac{7}{10}$ in. deep with a leather button to hold it closed. The shoulder belt was made of buff leather and was $1\frac{1}{2}$ in. wide, ending with separate straps to hook on to the pouch and a copper powder flask.

The 1850 *Ordnance Manual* described the same basic pouch, save that the end straps were to be 0.05 in. wider than before. However, the introduction of the rifled musket in 1855 made obsolete the special equipment for riflemen—with one exception—and rifle equipment was not mentioned in the 1861 *Ordnance Manual* or thereafter.

The additional piece of equipment needed by men armed with the M1855 rifle was a new belt to hold the sword bayonet which came with that rifle. This black waist belt was $42\frac{1}{2}$ in. long and $2\frac{1}{5}$ in. wide. It had a frog sewn to the belt on the left side, with a buckle which engaged a strap from the bayonet scabbard. The M1855 rifleman's belt was unusual in that it used a special brass clasp which did not bear a national insignia. Moreover, it had two brass loops which were intended to be used with the M1853 knapsack, although the two were rarely used together in actual practice.

Officers' Equipment

Officers had to buy their own equipment from the very first days of the US Army; and therefore, right up to 1910, their equipment—with the exception of most swords carried and belt plates worn—cannot accurately be said to have been totally 'regulation'. Essentially, the officer needed a sword, a haversack for food, and a canteen for water. On some campaigns he also needed a knapsack or blanket roll. In 1775 Americans generally copied the British Army, and British officers generally wore their swords under their waistcoats and sashes on waist belts. During the early part of the War, however, British officers began adopting shoulder belts, with a sword hanging from a belt passing from the wearer's right shoulder to his left hip over his waistcoat. Often a belt plate with some form of regimental markings was worn with this belt. American officers followed this trend, and by the end of the war the waist belt saw very little use as a sword belt. By far the majority of American officers wore black or white shoulder belts with their swords.

Otherwise, if they carried fusils, they wore cartridge boxes, often on waist belts, with tin tubes each holding one round, on the front of the stomach. Rations were carried in haversacks and water in canteens, both of the same kind as carried by their men. Spy glasses, if needed, were often carried in small leather tubes on shoulder belts.

This system of infantry officers' equipment lasted well into the 19th century, until 1821. At that time, bowing to popular pressure, infantry officers were authorised a waist belt on which to carry their swords in the field; but on parade they wore shoulder belts with which to carry the regulation foot officer's sword.

However, the regulation sword was a poor combat weapon; and many infantry officers, when they had the chance, obtained dragoon sabres, with heavy, curved blades, and white buff waist belts. This practice was officially recognised with the adoption of the M1850 foot officer's sword; it was heavier than the previous model, and made with a slightly curved blade, it came in a black leather scabbard with brass fittings that hooked to a black waist belt.

This Civil War infantryman wears the M1855 rifle belt, with its brass loops for the M1853 knapsack straps, and frame buckle. (David Scheinmann collection)

From that point, until the sword was finally abandoned by US Army officers, swords were worn on waist belts. Indeed, officers in Cuba in 1898 still wore swords, although in 1872 the frail M1860 straight-bladed staff and field officer's sword had been made regulation for all Army officers.

The dragoon sabre belts came with a shoulder strap that passed from a hook on the back, over the right shoulder, and hooked again on the left side for additional weight support. Most infantry officers' sword belts during the early years of the Civil War were made in this way; but most officers found that this belt hampered body movement, and removed

An American Officier

Many American officers of the War of Independence, such as this one drawn in New York in 1778, were armed with fusils as well as short swords. This officer carries his sword on a black shoulder belt with a metal tip and buckle worn over the coat, and a black cartridge box on a white shoulder strap on the other side of his body. (New York Public Library)

them. By the end of the Civil War, and thereafter, the shoulder strap was not worn on officers' sword belts.

Officers bought their own equipment, so in the years after the War of Independence they continued to use haversacks and canteens, often made of better materials than the issue items, and to patent designs. In the mid-19th century binoculars supplanted spy glasses or telescopes as being easier to use, besides affording three-dimensional vision. Officers who had binoculars

carried them in leather cases, not unlike the leather tubes they used for spy glasses but with two tubes.

Officers in the War of Independence were usually armed with spontoons—pike-like pole weapons—although some of them did carry fusils. Few carried single-shot pistols. In the years that followed, officers were armed solely with their swords. With the development of the multiple-shot pistol, however, they began to carry pistols for self-defence.

Since early model Colt pistols, the most common type available, were so heavy at the time of the Mexican–American War, few were then carried by infantry officers. But in 1851 Colt came out with the much lighter 0.36 in. calibre six-shot 'Navy' revolver; this saw action almost immediately as a private-purchase weapon among British officers in the Crimea, and good reports filtered back. Thereafter, most American infantry officers in the field began carrying pistols in holsters on their right hips, with their swords on their left. Until the advent of self-contained ammunition, officers wore the infantryman's issue cap pouch on the right front of the belt ahead of his holster; a black leather cartridge box for pistol ammunition was worn at the centre back of the same waist belt.

Experimental Systems

From the mid-19th century, individuals, usually serving officers, came up with various infantry equipment systems that were designed to be more comfortable, efficient, and healthy than the issued assortment of infantry equipments. These were generally patented before the inventor attempted to interest the Army in the system. After enough persuasion, the Army would often agree to test the system: a number, enough for one or more regiments, would be produced, issued, and then described by the unit commanders for the Army. If liked, the system would be adopted for general issue; if disliked, abandoned.

All were abandoned.

The Mann Equipment
Col. William Dalton Mann, 7th Michigan Cavalry, was the first in a parade of would-be system inventors. He patented a system of infantry

and cavalry equipment in 1863, with an additional patent for a method of fastening the knapsack added to his system in 1864. The system saw use in several regiments during the Civil War, but results were mixed, and it was not adopted.

Basically, the Mann infantry system featured a waist belt with a single large cartridge box worn square in front of the stomach. The box held 60 rounds, 40 on top and 20 underneath in two paper-wrapped packages. The box was further supported by means of braces that passed up the chest and around the neck; straps passed from these braces under the soldier's arms and attached to the knapsack behind, 'thus acting as a counterbalance to the other accoutrements,' according to Mann. The leather bayonet scabbard was permanently fixed to the left side of the waist belt by means of a large rivet around which it could be swivelled for comfort. Percussion caps were carried in the cartridge box.

There were two models of Mann infantry boxes: the M1863, which saw very little use, and the more widely employed M1864. The latter was an unusually large box, $7\frac{5}{8}$ in. long by $6\frac{3}{4}$ in. wide and $1\frac{5}{8}$ in. thick. The flap was 9 in. long and stamped with the Roman letters 'U.S.' within an oval which was marked 'COL. MANN'S PATENT RE-ISSUED JUNE 7TH 1863, E. GAYLORD MAKER, CHICOPEE, MASS.'

Since the oval brass US waist belt plate could not be used with the Mann system, a new buckle was produced shaped like an elongated 'Y', all three ends hooking into the waist belt.

Mann's 1864 equipment was made with a system for keeping the knapsack down when the soldier was jogging along; a short fly-strap on each side of the knapsack buckled to the belt.

The Mann equipment was issued for testing late in the War to the 4th and 15th New Jersey Infantry Regiments, and the 2nd Connecticut Heavy Artillery, acting as infantry. The 15th's historian recalled that 'The men liked the new arrangement, and no complaint from them was heard.' Men of the 2nd Connecticut, however, called the boxes 'belly trunks', and did not like them. The Army, after testing, did not adopt the Mann system.

The M1872 Equipment

In 1872 the Army ordered 5,000 sets of new infantry equipment for testing. 'These equip-

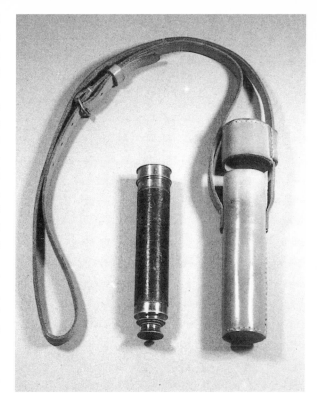

Many officers carried spy glasses in the late 18th–early 19th centuries. They came in brown (as here) or sometimes black leather cases. (Author's collection)

ments', the Chief of Ordnance reported in 1872, 'combine the knapsack, haversack, and canteen, with the cartridge-box, waist-belt, and bayonet-scabbard into one system, that can be used by the soldier either in whole or in part, as convenience or necessity may require; and his entire kit in complete marching order can be carried, it is believed, with ease and comfort, and without danger of impairing his health or strength.

'The Equipment consists of Waist Belt; Bayonet Scabbard, steel, with swivel frog; Cartridge Boxes, to hold each 24 Metallic Cartridges, carried in loops, (of two patterns for trial.); Valise to hold Clothing, with pouch under flap to receive two packages extra cartridges (440); Brace Yoke; and Coat Straps.'

The scheme was to use one cartridge box, square in the back or on the right front hip, for peacetime duty, and two on active service. Each box, designed by Col. P. V. Hagner, held 24 rounds of 0.50 calibre ammunition. The brace yoke would be used only when both boxes were carried, to support the added weight. The valise was to be attached to

the brace yoke—which formed an 'X' at the back—at the bottom of the 'X', just above the waist belt. It would hold trousers, shirts, a spare pair of boots, a blouse, socks, drawers, brushes, comb, and a towel. The overcoat and blanket would be carried rolled up and secured by a pair of leather straps in the centre of the back, fastened to the brace yoke, with or without the valise being used.

A haversack could be hooked to the left side of the waist belt. It included 'two sacks, in the larger of which the bread is carried and the other the sugar, coffee, etc. etc., in separate small bags. Under the flap is a pocket for the meat can, which will contain four days' rations of pork or of condensed meat. This can may be also used if necessary to boil coffee, and the cover for a drinking cup.

'A Canteen of Tin, covered with woollen cloth is also issued and will be worn attached to the Braces, or over the shoulder, as may be preferred.

'On the march, the soldier may unclasp the Waist Belt Plate at times, and thus give himself temporary relief without detriment to the stability of the load.'

The system was tested and rejected in 1874.

The Palmer System

The Palmer Infantry Brace System, which supplanted the M1872 equipment in testing, was patented by 1st Lt. George H. Palmer, 16th Infantry Regiment, in 1872. It included a waist belt plate designed by Col. Hagner, who commanded the Watervliet Arsenal. The system, very similar in appearance to the 1872 equipment, began trials in 1874.

It used an ordinary M1851 non-commissioned officer's belt with a rectangular brass belt plate bearing the Roman letters 'US' within an oval. A loop was cast to the left side of the belt plate, with another loop cast to the keep worn as part of the belt. A McKeever box was worn on either side of the belt plate. Black leather braces passed over the soldier's shoulders, forming an upside-down 'Y', one set of straps hooking on to the belt plate loops

The line officer's sword was usually worn, after the waist-belt replaced the shoulder belt, supported by a strap across the right shoulder. This Civil War Pennsylvania Bucktail captain also has a cap box on his right front hip, with apparently a pistol on his right side which cannot be seen. (David Scheinmann collection)

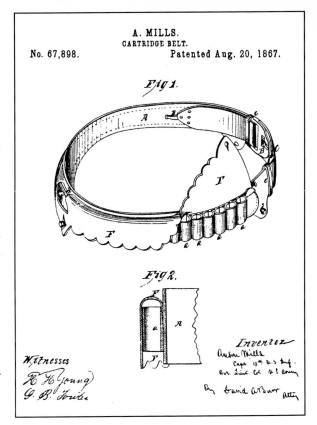

The original Mills belt, according to this patent drawing, included cartridge loops sewn on an M1851 belt and covered with thin leather flaps over every six loops.

and the other to two large sack-like haversacks, one serving as a knapsack, which hung on either side of the soldier's body.

The system saw only brief use in various trials before being abandoned.

The Metcalfe Magazine

It was also in 1872 that the Ordnance Department asked Capt. Henry Metcalfe to develop 'a suitable detachable magazine for the Springfield musket.'

Metcalfe used a block of 'white wood' $6\frac{1}{8}$ in. by $1\frac{1}{16}$ in. by $2\frac{1}{23}$ in., bored with ten 0.45 calibre holes in the top and with a wire loop attached to each end. This block, filled with metal cartridges, would be attached to the right side of the newly adopted 45/70 breech-loading rifle. The front loop would snap into an opening cut in the lower barrel band, while the rear one would engage with a stay pin set in the stock. Each block was to be loaded in an arsenal with cartridges which would then be covered by cardboard pasted to the block sides and

The M1872 experimental equipment included braces and a pair of cartridge boxes (left), and a blanket roll above a valise, with a haversack worn on the left side (right).

Pte. Charles Johnson Post, 71st New York Infantry Regiment, described wearing it in 1898:

'Its center was a canvas box about the size of the Civil War knapsack, which would hold just about a quart bottle comfortably with some space left for socks, shaving materials, and a deck of cards or so. The blanket was formed into a long roll across the top of the pack and down each side. . . . Beneath the Merriam pack were two more straps (in addition to the three holding the blanket roll). These were for one's rolled overcoat. . .

'Incidentally, the Merriam pack had two hickory sticks at each side fastened to the two upper corners of the pack. The other end fitted into the end pockets of a half-belt, which rested below one's kidneys. The Army believed that took the load off a soldier's shoulders. We carried the Merriam packs on our kidneys, and the leverage of the sticks pulled our shoulders back so that we were perpetually being pulled back downhill with the swing of leverage in each stride.'

In use, canteens were slung over the blanket roll,

The 1874 Palmer infantry brace system included braces with two McKeever boxes (left), with two valises worn behind in which clothing and food were stored (right).

varnished for protection. The soldier would rip the cardboard off to reveal the cartridges when the magazine was used. Metcalfe also cut down an M1855 cartridge box so it would hold four magazines, two inside and two on the front. A year later the Ordnance Department had Metcalfe change to an eight-round magazine. At around that time he replaced the wire loops with spring steel snaps.

The system was not adopted after testing in 1873, but was again tested in 1874. At that time Metcalfe changed the boxes so that they could be carried on a waist belt which he also designed. The belt plate was made up of a wire that formed the letter 'S' on its side, rather like the British 'snake buckle', with a wire 'U' soldered to it.

The Army ordered 34,692 Metcalfe magazines for testing—a mannikin displayed at the Centennial Exposition in Philadelphia in 1876 wore these magazines—but the system was never adopted Army-wide.

The Merriam Pack
Still the search for better infantry equipment continued. Col. Henry Clay Merriam's knapsack/haversack system was tested widely, starting in 1874. Soldiers unfamiliar with it called it the 'Merriam pack'—those intimate with it, the 'murdering pack'.

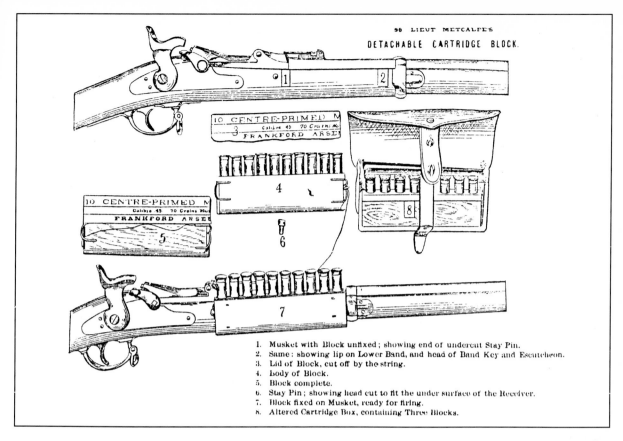

1. Musket with Block unfixed; showing end of undercut Stay Pin.
2. Same: showing lip on Lower Band, and head of Band Key and Escutcheon.
3. Lid of Block, cut off by the string.
4. Body of Block.
5. Block complete.
6. Stay Pin; showing head cut to fit the under surface of the Receiver.
7. Block fixed on Musket, ready for firing.
8. Altered Cartridge Box, containing Three Blocks.

hanging square on the top of the pack flap over the overcoat roll.

Merriam packs were abandoned in Florida before the Cuban invasion; they had never been adopted in US service, although New York's National Guard used them.

The Dodge System

First Lt. Charles Dodge, Jnr., 24th Infantry Regiment, focused his attention on the blanket roll. Recognising that soldiers preferred the blanket roll to the knapsack, although the Army felt that it cut off chest and back ventilation and restricted chest movement, he patented a new blanket roll system in 1892.

Under Dodge's plan, an ordinary blanket roll was made on a slender yoke of bent wood, some 5 ft 4 in. long. An adjusting rod and laces were used to fasten the ends after the yoke had been fitted to the individual soldier. The haversack strap then ran over the blanket roll, away from the soldier's body, and kept in place by means of studs set in the back and front of the yoke. The canteen strap passed around and just inside the blanket roll straps on the

These Metcalfe 'magazines'—cartridge blocks—were snapped on to the side of the .45/70 rifle for quick loading. Spare blocks were carried in special cartridge boxes worn around the waist belt.

yoke. A steadying strap on the yoke adjusting rod hooked to the waist belt so that some of the load was carried on the waist.

After trials, the wood in the yoke was replaced by spring steel, and the canteen was once again worn over the haversack instead of being attached to the blanket roll. Final trials of the Dodge system were made in 1909, by which time a better system was already on the drawing board.

The Plates

A: Infantryman and Officer, 1780
These infantrymen are clad in the uniform prescribed in 1779. The private, who wears the red facings of Pennsylvania, Delaware, Maryland or Virginia, has a leather bayonet scabbard mounted in a white linen shoulder belt. The cartridge box is

Dodge Blanket Roll Support.

The Dodge blanket roll support system included the horseshoe roll, which the men liked, with a thin wood, later steel, brace to keep it away from the body for better ventilation. This illustration is from the 1927 Bannerman catalogue of used military goods, which included Dodge blanket roll supports.

taken from an original in a private collection, and is the preferred box of the Continental Army; it contains only the wooden block, however, without a tin underneath. Two different types of typical musket slings are also shown; a third type used a brass buckle without a tongue. The private's weapon is a British Army Short Land pattern Brown Bess.

The lieutenant, dressed in the buff facings of New York and New Jersey, wears his sword belt over his coat (although it was often worn under it, with a plain frame buckle). His sword belt plate is taken from one worn by the commander of the 3rd New York Regiment. He is armed with a spontoon and a typical light sword.

B: Infantryman and Officer, 1813
Although whitened buff-leather was preferred, most soldiers of the American War of 1812 received black leather belts. Wood canteens were also typical, but tin canteens of this kidney-section shape were issued in the Northwest Army in 1812, and have been dug up at Fort Meigs, Ohio. The knapsack is the Lherbette patent model, adopted in 1808. The private's weapon is an M1808 contract musket. The captain's silver shoulder belt plate is rectangular, with lipped corners, and with a central national eagle for a design.

C: Infantryman and Officer, 1832
The Black Hawk War (April–September 1832) found a small but well-equipped army. The cartridge box was an improved M1808; the ornate flap adopted in 1832 is shown in detail. The grenadier company sergeant's weapon is an M1816 musket. The captain wears a waist belt with an M1821 belt plate, worn at those times when waist belts were worn instead of the regulation shoulder belt, until replaced in 1851.

D: Infantryman and Officer, 1847
The waist belt had been made regulation for enlisted men by the Mexican–American War. The cartridge box shown in the detailed sketch was designed for the M1842 musket; it could be worn only on a shoulder belt. The implement pouch was used for musket tools and patches. Notice the maker's name, Dingee, stamped on the inner flap. The corporal's weapon is the M1842 musket. The first lieutenant is armed with an M1840 foot officer's sword worn from the regulation shoulder-belt with its rectangular plate.

E: Infantryman and Officer, 1857
The French influence was very noticeable in the appearance of the Army that went to Utah to ensure that Mormon citizens there obeyed US laws. The corporal wears the M1853 knapsack hooked, as it was designed to be, to the M1855 rifle belt. Steps in attaching the buckle to the M1855 rifle belt are shown in the detailed sketch. The corporal wears no percussion cap pouch since the M1855 rifle came with the Maynard primer, a device using a roll of paper caps within the lockplate mechanism, instead of copper caps. The captain is also in dress uniform, armed with the M1850 line officers' sword.

F: Infantryman and Officer, 1863
The field dress of the American Civil War infantry

6,000 Merriam Patent U. S. Army Knapsacks. Made with side braces and straps to cross the hips and supporting braces to take weight of load from the shoulders, leaving the chest low free from all constriction, so that coat can be opened without deranging the equipment. The pack is divided into two compartments for clothing and rations. Good, serviceable order. Price, 70 cents each.

6,000 Merriam Knapsack Packs, with blanket roll straps. Used only a short time. Highly recommended by U. S. Army officers and surgeons for its even distribution of the weight of the pack. Made of strong brown canvas, with leather straps. N. Y. State Militia marking on cover. Illustration shows how the hip straps support the weight, the blanket and canteen carried on the pack. If any box knapsack is desired, then we can recommend this pattern as the best. Offer wanted for the lot of 6,000. All in good, serviceable order. Price of single knapsack, 70 cents. A very low price will buy the lot.

Two views of the experimental Merriam knapsack appeared in the 1927 Bannerman catalogue; (left) as worn, and (right) by itself. Note how the canteen was to be worn over the blanket roll that was wrapped around the body of the knapsack.

was plain but serviceable. The percussion cap pouches worn on the corporal's and first lieutenant's right front hips contain, as shown, an iron nipple pick. This particular model is an early one, with a shield-shaped outer flap; later examples had the flap and closing strap cut as one piece. The corporal's weapon is an M1861 Colt contract rifled musket. The first lieutenant has an M1851 Colt 'Navy' revolver in his holster. His sword is the M1850 line officers' model.

G: Infantryman and Officer, 1876

As though preparing for a guard-mount in the same year as the Battle of the Little Big Horn, this corporal wears a dress belt with a McKeever box, although the cartridge belt was preferred for field use. The backs of two types of McKeever boxes are shown; one slips over the belt, and the other was designed to be used with the braces of several experimental infantry equipment systems, such as the M1872 infantry equipment. The corporal's weapon is an M1873 rifle. The first lieutenant wears the M1860 staff and field officers' sword, made mandatory for all infantry officers in 1872.

H: Infantryman and Officer, 1898

Several variations of the M1887 web cartridge belt were in use during the Spanish–American War. The 'H' type belt plate was the first type; but to meet the sudden demand for gear for thousands of volunteers during that war, the Army adopted a simpler system using a simple brass wire fastening belt buckle, as shown in detail. The steel bayonet scabbard was worn hooked over the top of the belt as shown. During this period, too, the men started wearing their canteens and haversacks on opposite sides instead with the canteen on top of the haversack. The private's weapon is an M1898 (Krag-Jorgenson) rifle. The captain's M1896 0.36 calibre revolver is carried in a holster first issued around 1897.

Notes sur les planches en couleur

A Uniforme de 1779; liserés rouges de la Pennsylvanie, du Delaware, du Maryland ou de la Virigine, liserés en peau de buffle pour l'état de New-York et le New Jersey. Notez la bandoulière en tissu pour la baïonnette de ce soldat; et l'étui à cartouches caractéristique. Les officiers portaient souvent leur ceinturon, fermés par des boucles simples, sous leur manteau. Notez les différents modèles de bandoulières pour les mousquets.

B La plupart des soldats de la campagne de 1812–14 reçurent des ceinturons noirs. Les cantines en bois étaient courantes, cependant l'on vit ce modèle en étain dans l'Armée du Nord-Ouest. Le Havresac Lherbette a été adopté en 1808.

C Un soldat de la Black Hawk War—notez le rabat très orné de la boite à cartouches, introduite en 1832, et dont la conception a été améliorée. La plaque de ce capitaine, montée ici sur le ceinturon, se portait normalement sur la bandoulière d'ordonnance de l'épée entre 1821 et 1851.

D Le ceinturon était maintenant réglementaire. La boite à cartouches (détail) pour le mousquet de 1842 pouvait uniquement se porter sur une bandoulière. Ce caporal porte le mousquet de 1842, le 1er lieutenant l'épée de 1840, avec bandoulière réglementaire.

E Le havresac de ce caporal, qui date de 1853, est attaché à la bandoulière du fusil de 1855, dont la boucle de serrage est présentée en détail. Il ne porte pas de sac à poudre pour amorces étant donné que son fusil est équipé du dispositif d'auto-amorçage Maynard. L'épée de ce capitaine est un modèle de 1850.

F Dans les sacs à amorces, à droite sur le ceinturon de ce caporal et de ce premier lieutenant se trouve également un outil pour le mousquet. Le rabat des premiers sacs à amorces avaient une forme de bouclier et une bandoulière séparée comme ici; la bandoulière et le rabat des modèles plus récents étaient d'une seule pièce. Ce caporal porte un révolver Colt Navy, modèle de 1851 et une épée d'officier de ligne de 1850.

G Pour les gardes, le caporal a une boite à cartouches McKeever sur son ceinturon de grande tenue; il était normal de porter en campagne un ceinturon à cartouches à boucle. Les détails montrent deux modèles de boites à cartouches McKeever, l'une s'utilisant sur le ceinturon, l'autre sur les bretelles expérimentales. Ce soldat a un fusil de 1873, l'épée de 1860 pour les officiers d'état-major et de grades supérieurs qui devint réglementaire pour tous les grades supérieurs en 1872.

H Des variantes du ceinturon à cartouche de 1887 étaient utilisées; la boucle en 'H' d'origine fut remplacée par une attache métallique plus simple que l'on peut voir en détail. Notez que la gaine en acier de la baïonnette s'agraffe sur le ceinturon. Les soldats commençaient maintenant à porter la cantine et le havresac de côtés opposés plutôt que la cantine au-dessus du havresac. Ce soldat de deuxième classe porte un fusil Krag-Jorgenson datant de 1898; le capitaine le modèle de révolver .36 de 1896 dans un étui qui s'est tout d'abord vu en 1897.

Farbtafeln

A Uniform aus dem Jahre 1779 mit roten Aufschlägen die von den Bundesstaaten Pennsylvania, Delaware, Maryland oder Virginia benutzt wurden; lederfarbene Aufschläge wurden in New York und New Jersey verwendet. Bemerkenswert ist der aus Leinen gefertigte Schultergürtel für des Bajonett des Soldaten und der typische Patronenschachtel. Die Offiziers-Schwertgürtel wurden häufig unter dem Mantel getragen, verfügten aber über ein einfaches Koppelschloß. Auffallend sind die unterschiedlichen Musketenriemen.

B Die meisten Soldaten der Jahre 1812–14 erhielten schwarze Gürtel. Hölzerne Feldflaschen waren die Regel, dennoch verwendete man diese Blechflaschen bei der Nordwestlichen Armee. Im Jahre 1808 wurde der Lherbette Rucksack eingeführt.

C Soldaten aus dem 'Black Hawk War' (April–September 1832). Auffallend sind die verzierten Laschen, der im Jahre 1808 verbesserten Patronenschachtel, welche 1832 eingeführt wurde. Die Kapitänsgürtelschnalle wird hier am Hüftgürtel getragen. In der Regel ist sie an den vorschriftsmäßigen Schwertschultergürteln zwischen den Jahren 1821 und 1851 anzutreffen.

D Der Hüftgürtel war nunmehr vorschriftsmäßig eingeführt. Die Patronentasche (Einzelbild) der M1842 Muskete konnte nur an einem Schultergürtel getragen werden. Der Obergefreite ist mit der M1842 Muskete ausgerüstet und der erste Lieutenant mit einem M1840 Schwert sowie dem vorschriftsmäßigem Schultergürtel.

E Der M1853 Rucksack ist am M1855 Gewehrgürtel angebracht, dessen Koppelschloß detailliert abgebildet ist. Er besitzt keine Patronentasche für Zündütchen, da sein Gewehr mit dem 'Maynard-Selbstzündungssystems' ausgestattet ist. Der Hauptmann hat ein M1850 Schwert.

F Die Patronentaschen für die Zundhütchen, die vom Obergefreiten und ersten Lieutenant rechts vorn am Gürtel getragen wurden, dienten auch zur Anbringung von Gabelstützen. Anfänglich wurden die Patronentaschenkappen in der Form eines Schildes gehalten und hatten einen separaten Gurt, wie hier abgebildet. Spätere Entwürfe besaßen Kappe und Gurt, die aus einem Stück gefertigt waren. Der Hauptmann besitzt eine M1861 Colt 'Gewehr-Muskete'. Der Offizier hat einen M1851 Colt Navy Revolver und ein M1850 Frontoffiziersschwert.

G Für den Wachdienst war der Hauptmann mit einer McKeever Patronenschachtel ausgestattet, die an seinem Uniformsgürtel befestigt war. Während des Einsatzes wurde in der Regel ein lose sitzender Patronengürtel verwendet. Im Einzelbild sind zwei McKeever-Schachteln zu erkennen, eine für den Hüftgürtel und die andere für die experimentallen Schulterriemen. Der Soldat besitz ein M1873 Gewehr, der Offizier, das M1860 Schwert für den Stab und die Feldoffiziere. Im Jahre 1872 wurde dies für alle Offiziersränge vorschriftsmäßig eingeführt.

H Unterschiedliche M1887 Patronengürtel wurden verwendet. Das ursprüngliche 'H'-Koppelschloß wurde durch den einfacheren Drahtverschluß ersetzt, der detailliert abgebildet ist. Auffallend sind die Bajonettschiedenhaken am Gürtel. Die Soldaten trugen nunmehr Feldflaschen und Provianttaschen auf gegenüberliegenden Seiten und nicht mehr die Feldflasche über der Provianttasche, Der gemeine Soldat hat ein M1898 Krag-Jorgenson Gewehr und der Hauptmann einen M1896 .36 Revolver in einem Halfter, der erst ab ca. 1897 benutzt wurde.